Moments of Perfect Poise

Also by Gillian Telford, published by Picaro Press
An Indrawn Breath

Gillian Telford

Moments of Perfect Poise

Acknowledgements

Some poems in this collection, often in a slightly different form, have previously been published in the following literary magazines and e-zine: *Blue Dog Australian Poetry*, *Blue Giraffe 7*, *Eucalypt – a tanka journal*, *Eureka Street.com.au*, *Five Bells*, *FourW17*, *Poetrix*, *The Mozzie*, *Yellow Moon*.

Poems have also featured in the following anthologies: *Bird Before Landing* (Central Coast Poets Inc. 2002); *Crossing the Lino* (Wollongong Poetry Workshop 2003); *Ask the Rain* (Poets Union Inc 2004); *Suburbs of the Mind* (Central Coast Poets Inc. 2004); *The Best Poems of January, 2006* (Wollongong Poetry Workshop 2006); *Sun & Sleet* (Poets Union Inc. 2006); *the honey fills the cone* (Newcastle Poetry Prize Anthology 2006); *Mood Cumulus* (Central Coast Poets Inc. 2006); *The Cows Have Been There The Whole Time* (Bundanon Poetry Workshop 2008).

'The Pear Tree Dance' was commended in the 2004
Henry Kendall Poetry Award.

'The Rush' was highly commended in the 2007
Tom Collins Poetry Prize.

'Exotic' received an honourable mention in the 2008 Inverawe Outdoor Poetry Competition.

I have been privileged to have worked with many fine poets through the Wollongong/Bundanon Residential Poetry Workshops and would like to express my gratitude to Ron Pretty, Jennifer Harrison, Brook Emery, Michael Sharkey, Kevin Brophy, Judith Beveridge, Susan Hampton, Deborah Westbury, Jan Owen and Lauren Williams for sharing their skills and experience so generously.

I would also like to thank Beverley George for my tanka initiation and fellow poets on the Central Coast and elsewhere for their friendship and encouragement – in particular, Mary Hawthorne, my first mentor.

Moments of Perfect Poise
ISBN 978 1 74027 507 1
Copyright © text Gillian Telford 2008
Cover images: Robyn Bellamy • Cover design: Simone Hale

First published 2008
Reprinted 2015

GINNINDERRA PRESS
PO Box 3461 Port Adelaide 5015
www.ginninderrapress.com.au

Contents

At the Barre	9
Edge	10
Remembrance Day, 1949	11
The Rush	13
My Parish, 1954	15
Majorca, 1957	16
Observed in the Cafeteria Queue	17
Passage	18
A Private Geography	19
position in space	20
Watermark	21
Italian Mirror	22
September Synchronicity	23
tanka	24
All Night it Blew	25
Interred	26
The Pear Tree Dance	28
Nesting Time	30
tanka	31
Letter To The Editor	32
Midsummer Night	33
Early Warning	34
Some Rooms	35
Sayonara	41
Causeway	42
For Ken	43
The Colour of Japonica	44
Exotic	45
Relativity	47
The Dinner Party	48

Hunted	50
Combustion	51
Sweet Talk	52
The Tenant	53
Eavesdropping	54
Train Ride	55
Residential	57
with beating wings	58
tanka	59
Sunday morning	60
The Lifting	61
Dance	62
On Meeting Giacometti	63
Ferruginous	65
(i) Near Four Mile	65
(ii) Ferruginous	67
(iii) Weathered	68
painted smile	69
Solace	71
the boardwalk	72
Plans for Retirement	75
tanka	76
Winter Solstice	77
tanka	79

for my daughters Kristy and Simone
and my grandchildren
Tabitha, Harry, Sebastian, Imogen and Zachary

At the Barre

as if a visiting ballet-mistress
had rapped her cane
the tree ferns lift
their feathered skirts
arch and sway
then touch the forest floor

cabbage tree palms
rustle and shiver
throw wayang shadows
on the sandstone walls

from the undergrowth
comes a great commotion
        the tips of bracken ferns
wave and bend
as a trio of wrens emerge
fluffed and plumped up

the lyrebird
follows the wind

Edge

Rounding the headland,
the wind is left behind
to sweep the open bay.

Sandstone cliffs rise,
strata sliced, pastiched,
like fine Italian wafers.

Far below, the sea
plays bully boy with stranded rocks
then shakes itself, dogged.

The path veers inward,
becoming secretive with bush and vine
ocean surge now muted.

Here, the silence has
a whispering voice, stray down-draughts
menace the grasses

then all at once, I'm a child again:
crawling forward, Indian file,
coded signals from hand to hand,

moving with stealth
through forbidden territory,
every sense stretched

by the fear of discovery;
always
living by the dare,

going too close
to the edge.

Remembrance Day, 1949

She never came to church
or wore a hat
but every Sunday would send us off,
clutching our pennies for the collection,
while she sat by the fire
and listened to the radio serial.

One day a year
she'd appear in a fitted black coat,
a large black hat
not quite hiding her red hair,
with a scarlet poppy
blazing from her lapel.

She'd lead us off to church –
       three daughters
lined up beside her –
and she'd glare
if we made faces at each other
or dropped our hymn books.

You could see people looking at us,
hear them, from the pews behind
whispering '*poor little mites*'
while she'd sit there,
sometimes touching her eyes
with a white lace handkerchief.

When I was older, I realised
that the day she donned her poppy,
was the one day of the year
when she could play
the tragic young widow,
instead of being a woman replaced
by someone quite plain.

The Rush

Lace tight your white leather boots
wind the long ends around and around
now stand
– oh so tall on your high silver blades –
walk with the swagger you've practised at home
step on the ice with a nonchalant air –
      you're away

Saturday afternoons
the restless circling
gliding and weaving
now in now out
sharp-edged turns and lifting skirts
blades through ice
the rush
      whispers and intrigues
approach avoid
easy to flirt then skate away
or show your male strength
on a stop-dead blade

You didn't belong
if you had to hire –
exchange a ticket
for ugly black boots
scuffed and fetid
too big or too small
      you didn't belong
if you clung to the edge
      now and then daring

the blade-slashed corner
praying
they wouldn't cut a petulant flurry
to send you flying
scarlet with shame

In the centre
the stars kept spinning
knowing we circled
outside their orbit

I lace tight my white leather boots
wind the long ends around and around
then stand tall
smooth my skirt over my hips
step on the ice with a nonchalant air –
      I'm away

My Parish, 1954

I would know
that the tedium of Sunday matins
was almost at an end when
the droning tones of the vicar
became charged with righteous zeal
as the Marriage Banns were declaimed
for the *first, second or third time.*

From a pew below the pulpit
I thought I could see a tinge of warmth
creeping over his pallid cheeks
as one after another
spinster of this parish
was named before us
and we were exhorted
to search for *cause*
to denounce and expose
any *just impediment to their union.*

My pulse would start to race
and my mind fill with images
of suspendered thighs
and reddened lips,
of stifled giggles
and the Moulin Rouge.

The ladies of my parish
bore no resemblance
to spinsters.

Majorca, 1957

After she returned that summer,
she often lay on the couch, both hands
clasped behind her head, staring into space.

> Sometimes she'd stretch out a leg
> and turn her ankle
> as if admiring her soft leather sandals.

Behind her, the record-player
filled the room with disturbing music.
She told us this was called *flamenco*.

> Voices cried out against guitars
> as if in pain. Were men or women singing?
> Clapping hands pursued the rhythm,

feet stamped echoes in reply;
then castanets picked up the lead,
wood driven on wood

> until our world was reeling.
> On the record covers, we saw
> haughty, dark faces, tiered and ruffled skirts

held high to the knee,
black mantillas and buttoned shoes,
crimson satins like blood.

> After she returned, that summer,
> our mother smiled and laughed.
> Behind her back, we frowned.

Observed in the Cafeteria Queue

It's a childish ritual –
a game often played
elder sister
        younger brother
waiting together – filling in time

She stands behind him
hugging a tray
then takes a step forward –
over and again
with quiet insistence
she nudges her miniskirted hip
against his side

His face stays blank
        he studies the menu
while his body
blocks
and deflects
her every move

Like lion cubs
they jostle –
claws of pubescence
barely sheathed

Passage

Our mother wanted few reminders
from the life she was leaving
so when she brought us across the world
– three extra stamps
on her £10 (ten-pound) right of passage –
almost everything was left behind

My childhood then was closed
and locked into a leather writing-case –
secure beneath hidden flaps and pockets
I'd keep the key around my neck
to guard my changing life

Letters folded and re-folded
The Catcher in the Rye
a red exercise book filled with French verbs
pages of poems copied in ink
jazz and ballet programmes in shining covers
autographs gleaned from stage-door hours

And now the children of those children
are raising children of their own
but the bones of it all – the passions –
had already been marked out
when choices were made
to take from the old and bring to the new
only the most precious

A Private Geography

'Quinquireme of Ninevah from distant Ophir…' – John Masefield, 1910

Like an incantation
you murmur their names
over and again
        that's how it starts

It's a private geography
with personal ciphers
        whisper this name
and you're smaller than a pebble
in the bed of the Kali Gandaki river

Repeat another –
you find yourself kneeling at a stone embrasure
watching the waters of the Bosphorus
lap the shores of your palace

Or from the crowd a word spirals
        the axis spins –
now you're a black-veiled penitent
walking in procession for *Semana Santa*

But what of those words
that send you climbing
to where vultures straddle updraughts
on the spread of their wings
and you're moving in mist
at the rim of the clouds?

It's murmuring their names
that binds you

position in space

day by day
imperceptibly
I am weathered
becoming as silver-blurred
as sticks and twigs
that drift from tree tops
        then float
in vine-tied suspension
or geometrical absurdity
until they find a harmony
of air and space
with moments of perfect poise

living here
changes me

Watermark

Last night you came
disguised as Woman
in broderie anglaise petticoats.

With haughty wrists
you held them high
and danced a wild fandango

then dipped them low
and ran the full length of the beach
laughing

as you flung sweet spices behind you
to leave cinnamon traces
where your skirts had trailed

and tease us earth-bound seekers
who follow tide marks
and ponder mysteries at dawn.

Italian Mirror

In a time
as spare and lean
as a picked bone
your rococo extravagance
beguiles me

If I let a finger trace
the scrolls and curlicues
of your gilded frame
I find myself returning
to Florence
        to stand small
before Ghiberti's bronzed doors

You suggest reflection
        invite me to re-cross
small surfaces of joy
        See – there's the adventuress
slipping into Venice
on the early *vaporetto*
        now it's the dreamer
moving towards
the towered mirage
of San Gimignano

You catch my eyes
        those yearning eyes
in bevelled fragmentation

September Synchronicity

Grief
moves
from one skyline
to another

finds white sails
a great hall
an audience
waiting

youth
dressed in black
sing
with pure voices

one
follows another
the first again
then the other

polyphony creates
haunting
tintinnabulation

music speaks
strings release pain

grief shifts

finds solace
in this
global threnody

On 11 September 2001, the World Trade Center buildings in New York
and part of the Pentagon, Washington, were devastated by terrorist attacks.
Between 31 August and 16 September 2001 the Australian Chamber
Orchestra gave subscription concerts in seven Australian cities. The program
included Pärt: *Cantus in memoriam Benjamin Britten*; Takemitsu: *Death and
Resurrection*; Schubert: Quartet in D minor *Death and the Maiden*. On 13
September it was performed at the Sydney Opera House.

tanka

for Lois

you wipe away saliva
before it can seep
from the sides of your mouth –
I laugh and chatter
to quell my rising tears

halting words
as your body shuts down
link you with life –
if we destroy the forest
how will we hear the wind

All Night it Blew

the wind has washed the sand
clean of all footprints   all love letters
all seabirds' choreography

the wind has filled in
the burial mounds   toppled the castles
choked up childish kingdoms

the wind has buried the seaweed
the driftwood   the cigarette butts
the bladder bubbles of bluebottles

the wind has hollowed out
curves and shadows
fashioned shell shapes

and dimples   smooth rounded
softly moulded   miniature
dunes of the desert

Interred

All at once the grasping crowds
appal you –
an EXIT sign flashes
you open the heavy door
then hear it clang and slam behind you
now there is no way out
you must *enter* all who *exit* here
in the silence
you smell the stagnant air
        hear your lungs
suck the dry cement
see people running
up and down triangles
a repository of stairwells
remember Pythagoras
and the word hypotenuse
        you watch people opening doors
which close behind them
you want to call out
that you are there too
but your door says No Exit
you catch the panic ball
in your throat
and toss it aside
push down the bar
to open the next door
then another
you run up and down stairs
try every door

more doors
more stairs
more silent
    grey
        concrete
            passages

the panic ball
hits the far wall
and returns
you push hard on the bar
of the last double door
you scatter musicians
busking on the street
    the wide wide street
of your egress

The Pear Tree Dance

for Elizabeth Jolley – on first hearing of her illness

I have planted
a pear tree for you
Its roots are spreading

in the teeming chambers of your mind
where it will grow
to fill the space before your eyes

The birds will come and go
         you may smile a little
at the insistence of young shoots

Now you can sit
         watch how the light
plays with the dark

wait for that moment
when a drop of rain tips
from one leaf to another

You'll keep vigil through autumn
as your tree
strips to its bones

but when the last hoar fruit
can cling to the branch no longer
you'll ease back in your chair

and each spring
I will think of you
your bare feet treading the black earth

your pear blossom veil
drifting
as you come out to dance.

Ref. *The Newspaper of Claremont Street*, Elizabeth Jolley, 1981,
Fremantle Arts Centre Press

Nesting Time

The lyrebird is dancing,
From side to side he's prancing
And the bowerbirds are whirring in the lilly pilly grove.

The whip birds keep on calling,
Two notes as one, they're forming
And the bowerbirds are whirring in the lilly pilly grove.

The turkey's mound is growing,
He shows no sign of slowing
And the bowerbirds are whirring in the lilly pilly grove.

My daughter's busy painting,
In the nursery, all is waiting
And the bowerbirds keep whirring in the lilly pilly grove.

tanka

how gently
it leads us away
from vanity –
the curve
of a baby's cheek

Letter To The Editor

After Beslan: September 2004

Sir,

If they were my children
who had left for school
with first-day flowers
to be taught terror by cowards
in masks of shame
If they were my children
deprived of air and water
of sleep and my love
forced to gag on the dregs
of their own bodies' fear
If they were my children
who never came home

or my children
whose first days at school
now inhabit their eyes
then the final knife would turn
when before seven days had passed
their deaths and their lives
were reduced to one picture
of water bottles   teddy bears   wreaths and rubble
on one half
of page fifteen

Midsummer Night

you try in vain
to reach the whimpering child
        open door after door
of a house that once was home

from each window
the headland is the imprint
of a stricken beast
humping its shoulder
at the terrible sky
as maggots of blood
work through its flanks

columns of wounded trees
shuffle closer
        their sighs
the keening of night winds
        they reach out
with stiff black limbs
begging for the salve
of leaf-green wreaths

you scream
as the mare of the night
curls back her lip
on rotting teeth

a siren twists through sleep
with gimlet thread
then loops and yelps its way
around the bay

there is no rest
in this summer of fire

Early Warning

All day the air's been charged
           you're strung out like fence wire
flinching at intrusions

now there's the distant roll and rumble
of grumbling bombardment
the edgy foreplay of lightning

you can't hear
the quiet terror in the trees
for the frenzied calling of the birds

the world outside shuts down in mist
           as the first leaf bends
you feel the rending

then it comes in
           strong and hard
on the storm winds

and you're cut free

Some Rooms

'And tell me,...what have you in these houses? And what is it you guard with fastened doors?' – Kahlil Gibran, 1923

i   a kitchen

get a knife get a sharp knife test it on your thumb risk its menace take an onion a brown onion skin of watered silk dry wind rustle make a cut a deep cut slash the rings of symmetry slice and chop dice and hack set the juices flowing sniff a bit sniff a lot feel the dam wall breaking hear that song that same old song twenty ways to lose your lover now it's twenty-one

ii   a laundry

It was dark when I reached the laundry-shed – no power,
only torchlight and the moon rising over our campsite.

Late as it was, another woman was busy at the tubs; soaping, rubbing,
sluicing through a pile of clothes, her face pallid where my light swung.

We hadn't spoken before tonight, yet as we travelled ever further north,
I'd look up to find her watching me. When I'd smile in reply, she'd look away.

By the time we'd left even dirt roads behind, she was smiling back,
laughter lines returning to her tired eyes. Without words, something complicit evolved.

Now, we greeted each other as usual, worked side by side in silence
until she paused, turned to me with her hands still dripping and said

Did I hear you say you were on your own now, dear?

For some reason, I'd expected more than this from her;
was not prepared for platitudes or pity – not even the wisdom
of her years

but she wasn't waiting for me – she continued on, in rushes
and whispers,
as though there was not enough time and she was risking much.

It must be wonderful she said *being on your own –
coming on this trip on your own –* HE *didn't want to come –*

*he hates it but he wouldn't let me come without him;
you've seen him – heard him – he never stops –*

Still no reply was needed; only the freedom to talk – found
through shared ritual, our half-lit surroundings an intimate
confessional.

It was all right until he retired, she went on *I had the days to myself,
the housework and garden, my sewing – but now he's always there.*

*He never leaves me alone – not for a moment – he follows me, he interferes,
tells me what to do – can you imagine – things I've been doing all my life*

She stopped, looked down to the wet clothes; her bloated hands
starting once more to grab and twist, then turned back to me;

Some days – she whispered *some days
I can only get through by planning how to kill him.*

iii a bedroom

secret musk hint of thyme listen how the bodies rhyme
trace a shadow ripples form white-moon nights webs at dawn
avocado sliced and stoned fleshy sweetness aching wound
tango stepping arch and turn gliding melding tactile burn
hold the moment let it run sea-mist shivers touched by sun
cortège wheeling plumes of black drum-beats muffled end the
pact

iv a waiting room

His rooms were found in an aging terrace;
discreet enough she thought, making her way
up narrow stairs to where murmured voices
colluded behind closed doors and the day

seemed full of portents and the mystery
of whether she'd reveal herself to him.
As she waited, she grabbed a New Yorker,
disturbing the neat pile, needing some mayhem

to match her agitation, the chaos
of the thoughts she hoped to disentangle.
Sitting in the silence, she mourned her loss
of reticence and changed the diagnosis.

A gilt-edged mirror, spying from the wall,
watched as unmasked, she curled into a ball.

v   a consulting room

Lust has entered here
and taken it for its own.
You feel it crawling
from the pages of old books
like feasted silverfish;
smell its mildew on tasselled braid,
trace its stain on velvet chairs,
     watch it shudder as the street-light
stirs phantasms against the wall.

I see you crossing the rug
to sit at the desk where a small lamp glows
an island of hope defined by its warmth
you must hear them
the voices that fill the room
     calling from corners
whispering in the shadows
voice lapping voice
now woman now man

From the bookshelves
behind the desk, you feel observed
by those great men of lust –
Carl Jung and Sigmund Freud.
In such a room they tossed
ideas from one side to another;
analysed their 'big' dreams and symbols,
supported and revered each other
until the final schism.

vi a studio

The day after I'd started re-working this poem, I went into the city and made an unplanned visit to the Museum of Contemporary Art which was showing part of the 2004 Biennale of Sydney. Amongst the works was one entitled The Sofa of Jung *(Mario Rizzi – Italy). This installation was set in two rooms – Jung's Studio. You were invited to 'walk on the rug, sit at the desk, sit in the chairs, study the bookshelves…' On the desk were copies of two letters in German, signed by Jung and Freud. As you walked around, you could hear above you the taped voices of men and women, reading letters or possibly case notes with male and female voices overlapping from different corners of the rooms. I noted that the pieces of furniture were not authentic but chosen from local antique stores. I'm sure Jung would agree my visit was a perfect example of 'synchronicity' – a meaningful coincidence.*

vii a study

late afternoon sunlight
slides into corners
steals warmth from books
      sets their spines glinting

once more
I study the picture
behind your desk
and wonder why its frame
remains empty in my mind

as a parting gift
I unwrap one last dream –
release the images
set the night birds free

you stay with me but I lead the way
– show you their perches fashioned from ivory
        food bowls of porcelain fastened with jade
the celadon eyes waiting dull behind bars
the lift of wings in the flight towards dawn

Sayonara

Seabirds huddle
nursery cliques
screams of protest
peevish eyes

flapping flights
now and then
up a bit
down again

too much trouble
back to basics
peg-leg cuddles
drifting down

criss-cross cryptic
hopscotch cipher
waves of motion
ceaseless surges

tidal flight path
greets the sunrise
floods the claw-work
wipes the whiteboard

bird's-eye viewpoints
never published
detritus sweeping
out to sea

Causeway

On one side
the sea frets
in the wake of night-time rage
to find its sweetest waters
out of reach
abandoned to lie around in pools
pretending to be sky

A figure
dark against the light
steps on to the catwalk
        shields her eyes
struts forward
(first the pelvis then the chin)

The ocean moves
        with tidal lunge
traps her in space   spume
white-light   white-noise
designer-bubbled iridescence
salty   lip-licking applause

then rolls on inwards –
re-takes the dais
accepts due homage
reclaims its waters

For Ken

6/12/2004

We went to his memorial service
expecting him to be there
        filling the space
with his big presence
        telling us stories of love and life

I thought I saw him for a moment
as he waited in the wings
booming out directions through a megaphone
a glass of good red to hand

They had done their best
The text was crafted with love
and poetry
        but he wasn't reading it

Perhaps in this family
he was the only performer
        for no one there could match him

The Colour of Japonica

for RB

She arrives at my door
late one afternoon
bringing in from the cold
the warmth of laughter
and gifts for the house
      some good red wine
the first of her japonica

We sit by my fire
catch up on news
of movies and daughters
galleries and gardening
the politician we both despise
She gasps a little
with her first sip
of the wine I've been drinking
but murmurs something reassuring
about *hints of oak*

After she leaves
I toy with the blossoms –
their colours deepening
in the fading light
The thorny spikes resist arrangement –
displaying their buds
in random clusters
they twist and turn
until one artless veer
reveals their elegance

Exotic

She steals what she cannot have –
finds quiet paths to suit the season.

She knows each empty house,
the gates that open without a sound,
the sliding point of every half-nailed paling.

They say she leaves early, walking down
through pink-tipped lilly pilly and blueberry ash;

she-oak and hakea, sassafras, pittosporum:
past hibbertia twining around old man banksia;
tree ferns waiting with frond-clenched fists.

The neighbours watch her now; she's earned a reputation.
Look what she has – they say – *Isn't that enough?*

Some of them rise before dawn,
seem not to hear
the cockatoos' derision, the kookaburras spreading the joke.

Then she appears –
out of the sea-mist, like a wayward nymph,
garlands in her hair, face buried in blooms.

What have you got this time they call,
prepared to shame her, surprised
when she answers with a smile.

Look she says *smell these* –
holding out bundles of sweet honeysuckle,
the first jasmine of spring.

They are so wicked but I can't resist them –
if I grew them here – they'd sucker and spread,
clamber and strangle –
so I fill my house with stolen weeds.

Relativity

Cicadas stun, then mask all sound
        turn foreground to background
so even a yelping dog seems mellow.

Your small entrance
catches my eye –
elegant markings, stately mien:

as you make your way forward
with tiny flicks of the tongue
and turns of the head, your tail is immaculate.

An ant crosses your path
and suddenly I'm watching
with your blinking eyes

as the legs of the chair
become tree trunks
a leaf, shifting in the breeze

is a log to be dodged
and the ant
has the jaws of a tiger.

The Dinner Party

the bubbles of her voice are floating over the bench-top and bouncing off the dinner-guests i start to duck as i see them moving towards the shiny-bright bali birds swinging on their mobile too late too late POW a million bubbles hit a million birds they crash and shatter into a million glass beads now they're eggs the coloured birds are laying coloured eggs i say a magic spell and now they're marbles i hold a marble up to my eye but its swirls make me dizzy i look at my mother round the edges of my marble the marble is the coloured bit of my eye my eye is blind i have a special eye which sees from the white bits sometimes they're light blue some peoples are yellow with red bloody bits at the corner like my aunt's i don't like her eyes

there's a light right above mum's head it's hidden in the ceiling the light's shining down on her hair it's all shiny and misty looking i've seen a picture like that on the wall at church a light coming out of a cloud and some birds and things she's looking up again and smiling at us all and my dad's looking at her with that funny sort of look on his face i'm going to look at something else

i'm looking through the leaves of the giant pot-plant if i move my head a little i'm a big cat in the jungle i'm watching them from my hide-out i can see them but they can't see me if they looked through the leaves very carefully they could see my shining marble eyes one red and one yellow but they're not looking they're all having a picnic around the water-hole laughing drinking and eating i get very hungry just before dark that's when i'll get ready to pounce i'm remembering all the things my mother taught me about hunting always wait she said always wait until they start drinking and eating be very quiet try not to wriggle too much or you'll disturb them once they've started then it's your turn when you take some food hold on to it tightly so you don't drop it or make a mess it's getting darker now i'm getting very hungry i'm almost ready they're all moving closer to the waterhole they're sitting down round the picnic table i'm stalking them now but they don't notice me behind them i'm moving right amongst them my mothers voice is a tiger roar and it's saying

help yourself so i do

Hunted

sometimes
when you're driving fast
on the freeway
        out in front
alone
late at night
you see the lights
of the pack
far behind you
closer
                coming closer
around bends
now the straight
catching up
pairs of yellow eyes
in unison   in pursuit
unrelenting   closing-the-gap
then you know
how it is
for a gazelle
losing ground

Combustion

She turned to him
        where he sat
        not quite touching her
to tell him about the play

Her words
flowed over him
erudite   polished
flecked with foam
from the side of her mouth
Though his eyes never left her
he heard nothing

I watched
what was happening
between them
the same way
I watch a wood fire
through soot-stained glass
see the writhing coil of gases
in those moments before
smoke becomes flame
and two forces flare
into one

then I remember
those times
when I've played
in the space of the place
between words

Sweet Talk

When he finally
kissed her neck
        in that certain place
around the periphery of the ear
        he murmured something
about the texture of peach skins

Later
he told her about fireworks
exploding
        against a night sky

She told him what happens
when you drop a pebble
in a pond filled with lilies
        and golden carp

When he left
he sighed that he would miss
        her sexy knees

She reminded him
that help was available
these days
for men
with commitment problems

Her teenage daughter
        flicked the fringe
from her eyes – said
that she wouldn't have let
him escape

and she believed her

The Tenant

He moved in last spring to the upstairs flat;
seemed pleasant enough and eager to please
but he had this way of stroking his cat

that left me with feelings of strange disquiet
as I watched the way she allowed him to tease.
He found summer hot in the upstairs flat

so often came down for a friendly chat
or a long, cool drink in the evening breeze
but he had this way of stroking his cat,

caressing her fur in this way then that,
which still left me filled with a vague unease.
Autumn was cool in the upstairs flat;

he lit a small fire, invited me up;
I was tempted to leave his hand by my knee
but he had this way of stroking his cat

till she'd writhe and coil on his Persian mat,
purring and growling with tightly closed eyes.
In winter I moved to the upstairs flat
for he had that way of stroking his cat…

Eavesdropping

They've been telling each other
their backpacker tales –
        swimming with dolphins,
cheap beaches in Thailand.

My well-trained ear
is shameless –
        has to eavesdrop, weave stories.
Now he's asking a question;
Would you like to go to Dakar?

She's Swiss-German
        of that I'm sure
and he's .. well he's too fluent
to pick in one.

Perhaps they've just met –
        she's wary…
I've been to Dakar three times already…

he's smooth…
correcting her comprehension –
*I didn't ask you
how many times you'd been to Dakar,
I said, would you like to go there?*

then adds without pause
or change of inflection
I'd like to go to Ethiopia

but they leave the train
at Murrurundi.

Train Ride

Two young men
sit in front of me
on this crowded train

        travelling first
        through long late sunlight
        now darkness.

                No more scenic
                reverie
                to look outwards
                is to look
                inwards

and mirrored images
conceal the night.
I hadn't noticed them before

        but one has become agitated.
        His ranting, his gestures
        disturb me.

                The other sits in
                silence
                and like a
                watching cat
                is perfectly still

until he moves,
flings back a seat
to face the carriage.

Cold eyes slide over me
then flicker to his mate
my perfect vulnerability.

                    Shots of
                    adrenalin
                    shorten each
                    breath. I'm
                    shocked by the
                    menace

one glance has revealed.
My station's next
but is it theirs too?

          I leave the train and watch
          from the crowd until each carriage
          is doused by the night.

                    They didn't get off,
                    I'm sure,
                    so why are there
                    footsteps
                    behind me now?

Residential

In the languor of late afternoon
a window propped wide pretends to cool
        permits the small sounds
of even smaller birds, fussing at the eaves
        a muted argument
        hangs
unresolved above the quadrangle
then bursting out against the distant traffic
an interchange of shouted banter
youthful laughter, slamming doors

and yet the train predominates
rattling and swaying along the escarpment
        slicing the world into *here* and *not here*
splitting the stillness with empty cries

this stolen time
        this interlude of focus
is drawing to an end

so why is it
that I'm flung
into nostalgia for the everyday
        caught unawares
by the notes from a violin
as they rise
        rest on my window ledge
and talk to me of home?

with beating wings

suggested by Li Po

in front of the mirror
        a white vase stands empty
your scarlet robe no longer swings
        behind the bedroom door

you are everywhere
        yet nowhere –

– only a hint of your essence
when I search for you at night
        soothing the ragged satins of your quilt

it is over

golden leaves tumble into the fountain
and the wild geese fly north

tanka

why choose the koel
as your messenger
all night it calls
but never finds the notes
to write our love-song

Sunday morning

the rain is easing now
all night its sounds have stippled sleep
         insistent   intrusive
playing with dreams

an early wind
swings in amongst the trees
sends branch-loads of showers
slapping down against the roof

you reach out
remember you're alone –
look up to where the skylight
frames the dawn
then watch as droplets merge
and slide a slow trajectory
down angled glass

The Lifting

What is it
about turning a scented wrist
that drives the pulse
to race against the bone?

Is it
the memories that cling:
       that shock of encounter
as if you've opened a wardrobe door
and breathed a forgotten life.

Or is it
a lost innocence of skin,
       that intimate delta
where blue veins
are vulnerable:

the hands, languid through air;
what eyes may say?

And who is it
who raises the wrists, so gently
turning each over,
       then back
while the white flesh
waits
for that uptake of breath?

Then was it you
who followed me all day
       and throughout that night,
begging to lift my wrists?

Dance

let's save the tango
for tonight's last dance
        after we've moved
with the rumba and the samba
        after we've learned the rhythms
of not-touching   not-looking
        after we've yielded
to the arrogance of a turned head
the message from an angled hip
        after we've found
we are swaying as one
through the silk-skirted air

On Meeting Giacometti

at The Art Gallery of NSW, 2006

(i)

    in profile
the power
of your *Monumental Head*
is greater than its name –

move full-face
and under this relentless gaze
    I am strangely disassembled –
a formalin frog of twitching muscles –
a specimen
light-pierced against black velvet

detachment peels
layer after layer
exposing the disorder of existence

now I open to your vision
locked eye to eye
we merge   we part

(ii)

I have a premonition of pursuit
    perhaps your *Walking Men*
are creeping up behind?
but when I turn
they are no closer –

suspended
between departure and arrival
        shoulders set
stilt legs weighed down by ponderous feet
        as though each step
must somehow earn release

(iii)

back in Saint-Paul it is summer now
        hot winds
sough through the pine forest
to spike the air with resin
        the empty courtyard
waits for its residents' return

yet in these airy rooms –
would you agree –
your figures seem at home
and have retained full mastery
of light and space
        their fragile limbs well earthed
        their greater selves set free
to roam in shadow play?

today I had the privilege
of meeting them alone
and though, like me, they're not gregarious
I feel compelled to come again

Giacometti: An exhibition of sculptures, drawings and prints by Alberto Giacometti (1901–1966), from the Maeght Foundation, Saint Paul, France and the AGNSW

Ferruginous

The following three poems were written as part of the script for Ferruginous, an audio-visual collaboration between some members of Central Coast Poets Inc. & the visual artist, Jeff Pickering, inspired by his photographic studies of abandoned cars. It was presented at the Peninsula Theatre, Woy Woy, on 24 November 2006 as part of the Cultural Laboratory Program sponsored by Gosford City Council.

(i) Near Four Mile

Only the crow
knows about loneliness;
        knows where it breeds,
the colours it wears.

Watch it fly
towards Jindabyne;
see where it struts,
what its white eye studies.

It will find you here,
the loneliness: it breathes
through the heat of the day,

draws you into its kingdom;
this graveyard of relics,
feeding on rust.

Now you must join
its solitary dance,
        grass skirts
bleached and fraying,

sway to the monotony
of abandonment
on a fly's listless drone,
then wipe from your eyes
the pathos of dust.

(ii) Ferruginous

fractured fragmented fissured in fusion fine feathered
filaments
ferrous finessing filigree framework fragile forms frescoed
fretwork frenetic flamboyant fiction forests of fungi
flood-lit fantastic Fiats and Fords lie fallow at Flynn's

(iii) Weathered

light plays on chrome
        a metal cross
        artless shrine
of grass and weed
        an off-road grave
stripped raw   peeled back
soft weatherings of time

painted smile

(i)

While he is in hospital, I sleep in his room,
surrounded by pirate paraphernalia,
crates of lego and growing mounds
of furry animals.
Dinosaurs prowl the walls, football heroes
are poised for the perfect goal
and when sleep eludes me
I lie and watch the planets
spin their luminescence above his bed.

Among the cards and gifts sent home
is a yellow balloon, with a painted face.
Tethered,
       its flight curtailed,
it turns in slow circles
to greet me each day with a counterfeit smile.
Breaking free,
it floats to the ceiling,
settles in a corner with its face to the wall

(ii)

Home for the day,
he runs in to find me – then points and shouts.

For now in the room,
       like some eerie stalker
the shrinking balloon is hovering behind me.

I move and turn but still it clings,
staying afloat on the air I displace.

He sees what is needed – heads straight for his toy box,
pulls out a cutlass and slays the pursuer.

With painted mouth twisting
        it crumples and falls –
he hoists it high on the tip of his sword.

We laugh and talk, we hug –
we glimpse the terror in each other's eyes.

Solace

(i)

Out of rhythm
and far from my own quiet spaces,
I discover the fountain:
> its voices lap my thoughts –
> subdue the inner sea.

Around me, wisteria writhes
and reaches out
as if to hide its knotted veins:
> from these depths a bird pipes out
with small, defiant notes.

Box-hedged, I breathe the humus deep,
> catch the yellow leaf
that drifts across my hand
and let the fountain's flow
re-set my metronome.

(ii)

Day after day of wind and rain –
> autumn's load spins down
to pile in saffron drifts.

Now the wisteria's sap has dried
and last week's potent wands
hang down in listless claws.

> But the bird still calls
from its sheltered perch;
the sun can penetrate the shade

while from my hidden seat
I hear the fountain lions
pour out their endless balm.

the boardwalk

Tamar Island Wetlands Reserve, 2007

(i)

a bleak waterway
when I first crossed to the island
many years ago

weeds and silt choked the estuary

water birds flew on
and barely skimmed the surface

broken reeds
struggled for footing in remnant pasture

a solitary bird hide
with cut-out walls to scan the empty sky –
was this where visionaries came to dream?

low tide exposed stark new timbers –
one and a half kilometres reaching out
over old levee banks and rivulets –
       a walkway still alien
       to its landscape

(ii)

this year I return
       stepping with care
over stained and seasoned boards –
       wire-covered in parts
against the treachery of slime and frost

now I enter a shifting world of reeds
that almost form an arch above my head –
    I hear tiny birds
chatter and scold as they dart in and out
        setting the seed heads swinging

look into the depths
and here is chaos –
vertical/diagonal/horizontal shafts
of reeds – *Phragmites australis* –
        like a festival of box kites
        disassembled

(iii)

on the island
traces of European settlement
are folded in time
    like the leaning plough
you find embalmed within an oak

move on to the far side and here
throughout its length
the main channel of the Tamar
ebbs and flows in tidal sweeps

near its mouth
the woodchip mills with gaping jaws
    strip chew and spit out forests –
while I walk
protestors gather in city parks
to march with banners –
promises are processed – pulped

(iv)

as the tidal waters drain
> all is witch-talk   ooze and suck
> when there is a lull in the wind –

a break from endless gossip with the reeds –
every sound is liquid

now the water birds swoop low to feed –
chestnut teal sieve the shallows
like teams of weekend lawn mowers bent to the task –
a white-faced heron repeats its image in reflected sky
while beneath the bridge
> a black swan spins against the current

in a taffeta flare

'At just over seventy kilometres, the Tamar is the longest estuary in Australia. It contains many wetlands, the most important being the Tamar Island Wetlands. Practices such as drainage, farming, engineering, duck hunting and shooting have now been phased out.' – Tamar Island Wetland Centre Brochure, 2007 – Parks & Wildlife Service, Tasmania

Plans for Retirement

We had a game
my friend and I
        turn after turn
over and over
we'd swing through the air

backwards and forwards
bare legs pumping
        higher and stronger
                stronger and higher
until we were part of the sky

then with thudding heart
and cheeks of fire
we'd let go the chains –
        fling ourselves
        towards the line scratched on the earth
always trying to cross that line

so watch me now Sal
it's my turn

tanka

silenced by height
a plane trails vapour
across pure sky –
squealing with joy
fruit bats swing into blue

Winter Solstice

In the cave of late afternoon
I am knitting –
real wool
travelling between my fingers
        the slide of metal on metal
        the warmth and weight
of a growing garment
        the tug and play
of needles and yarn

today
is the shortest day of the year
        from the windows
the forest is still –
ink-sketched foliage
not yet merged with the fading sky
and even the birds are silent

every sound has its place –
        jazz
curls into corners
        the slow combustion stove
shifts its black cladding
with mutters and sighs
        deep in its embers
the parted lips of the banksia cone
swell and blush
like some whorish fantasy

then images surface –
young hands outstretched
with thumbs raised high
holding long skeins of wool
    keep them apart a voice instructs
as older hands wind and weave
to conjure up a perfect sphere

the longest night begins

tanka

there is more space
in a frond of maidenhair
than substance –
what is not said, or not yet said
writes the truest poem

all at once
I crave newspaper, kindling
a lighted match –
such strange intuition
knowing when to move on

www.ingramcontent.com/pod-product-compliance
Lightning Source LLC
Chambersburg PA
CBHW062149100526
44589CB00014B/1756